RUSSELL TOVEY + ROBERT DIAMENT

Foreword by Olivia Colman

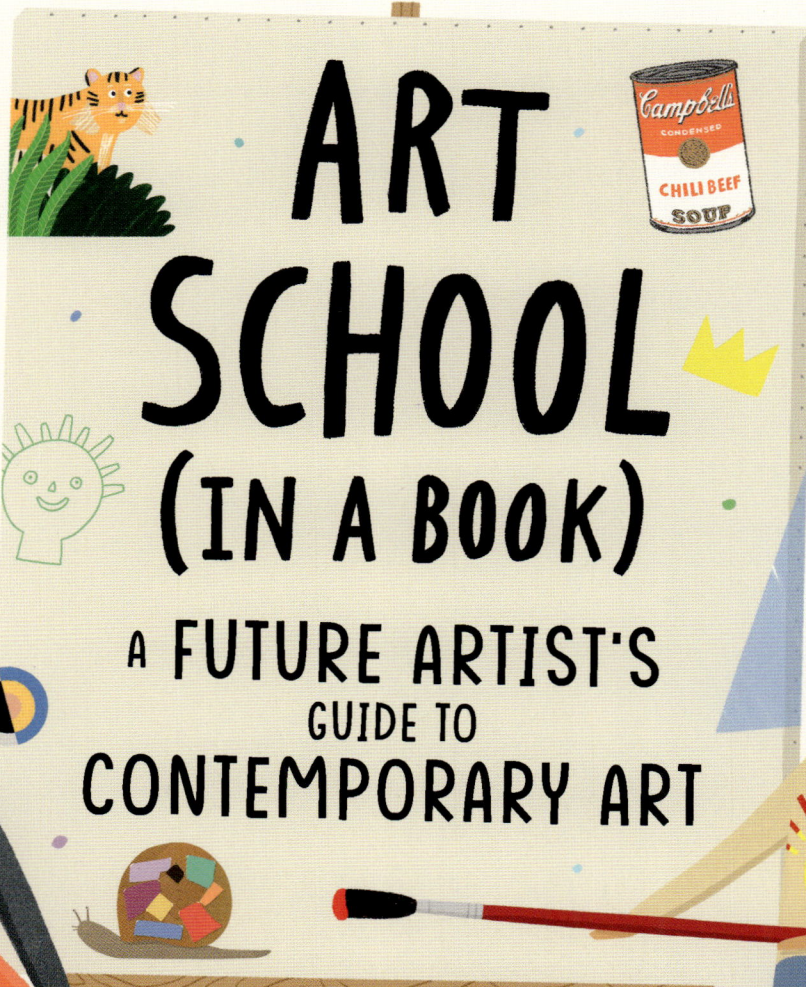

Campbell's
CONDENSED
CHILI BEEF
SOUP

ART
SCHOOL
(IN A BOOK)

A FUTURE ARTIST'S
GUIDE TO
CONTEMPORARY ART

Rose Blake

LAURENCE KING

Thank you

Russell and Robert would like to thank all of the artists included in this book for allowing us to share your inspiring artworks and stories. We are very proud to have your work included here.

Special thanks to all the teachers around the world who are supporting art education and creativity in all its forms.

Thanks to our editors at Hachette, to our collaborator Susie Hall who helped us during the making of this book, to Olivia Colman for her beautiful foreword, to our team at Independent Talent – Louise, Grace, Zach and Paul, to our Margate family Carl Freedman and Tracey Emin for constant support, to our pets Rocky, Window and Doorway, and finally much love and gratitude to all of our *Talk Art* podcast listeners around the world for being so loyal.

Thanks to all our friends and families who have always encouraged our enthusiasm for art, especially our mums Carole and Judith.

Most of all, thank you to all the future artists reading this book. We hope you are feeling inspired and we look forward to seeing the art you create!

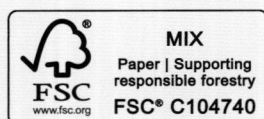

LAURENCE KING

LAURENCE KING
First published in Great Britain in 2025 by Laurence King

ISBN: 978-1-510-23141-2
E-book ISBN: 978-1-510-23143-6
10 9 8 7 6 5 4 3 2

Printed in Italy

FSC
www.fsc.org
MIX
Paper | Supporting responsible forestry
FSC® C104740

Laurence King
An imprint of
Hachette Children's Group
Part of Hodder and Stoughton Limited
Carmelite House
50 Victoria Embankment
London EC4Y 0DZ

An Hachette UK Company
www.hachette.co.uk
www.hachettechildrens.co.uk
www.laurenceking.com

The authorised representative in the EEA is Hachette Ireland, 8 Castlecourt Centre, Dublin 15, D15 XTP3, Ireland (email: info@hbgi.ie).

Foreword by Olivia Colman

Two things in life are guaranteed to brighten your day – to open your eyes and give you a fresh, funny, moving and hopeful perspective on things: kids and art. (And of course dogs. But that's a different book.)

So, what better than to combine the two? To discover the wonder of art anew through a child's eyes . . . and to discover the wonder of children afresh, through a shared joy in art.

And for you kids – what better way to help your grown-ups learn really important things like 'your child can tidy their room TOMORROW', than by sitting them down and showing them some lovely pictures?

Because through all of this, art will remind us of the most important thing of all: that beauty is within all of us. (And in dogs.)

Hello! It's a pleasure to meet you.

Who are we?

We are   **Russell**   and   **Robert.**

Welcome to our art adventure!
We love art and want to share with you the many reasons
why it brings us so much joy.

Art can be many things – it can be numbers, letters, pictures, lights and even noises! Art is also expression, and one of the most powerful things we can learn as we grow up is how to express our feelings and how to celebrate the things that bring us joy.

Come journey with us to explore this magical world!

What is art anyway?

Humans have been on this planet for over 200,000 years. How do we know this? Because of the art that has been left behind. If you go into any museum in the world, you will see objects that are probably much older than you. Older than your parents, even – older than your grandparents!

Creating things has always been important to humans. Firstly, for survival – they needed to make vessels and tools to cook with, store things in or to prepare food with. But it wasn't all about necessity – humans also created cave paintings, in order to communicate and keep a record of their daily lives.

Art connects to everything. Think of this book you're holding. It was designed by a book designer who studied art. Think of the chair you're sitting on. It was also designed by someone who studied art. Look around the room you're in. The room was designed by an architect who – guess what? – probably studied art. Art is all around us – it's even within us – and we're going to show you just how fun and rewarding it can be to express your artistic vision.

What can art do for you?

Art can tell a story by showing us our past, present and future. Every time we pick up a pencil, crayon or paint brush, we are following in the footsteps of the greatest storytellers who have ever lived. By looking at art, we can learn more about ourselves. Many artists have shown us their joy, sadness and frustration through their creativity, because artists make art about the people, places and things that they love. We might be able to imagine what an artist felt when they created their work – we might even feel the same. And when we recognise ourselves in someone's art, that artist helps to reveal to us more about who we are.

We'd like to share some of our favourite artworks with you. They're all different, and each one holds a special place in our hearts. Let the art fun begin!

Henri Matisse

The Snail (1953)
286.4 cm x 287 cm
Abstract

This colourful artwork by French artist Henri Matisse is a collage made with paper, gouache (a water-based paint) and scissors. Matisse was nearly ninety years old when he created it, and his poor health meant that he couldn't paint as much as he would have liked. So, he started cutting coloured paper into different shapes and collaging them together to make artworks. *The Snail* is very big and was designed to be hung up on a wall.

Can you see how the artist has shaped the colours into a shell in the middle of the paper?

It doesn't look exactly like a snail, but Matisse wanted the image to become clearer the more people looked at it – this is called abstract art. He chose very bright colours. Would you do the same?

Do you like that it isn't an exact copy of a snail? Can you imagine other insects or creatures that the artist could have made with these colours? Perhaps try collaging a butterfly with different pieces of colourful paper. You can make the wings in different shapes and shades. And remember, it doesn't have to look exactly like a butterfly, because this is abstract art.

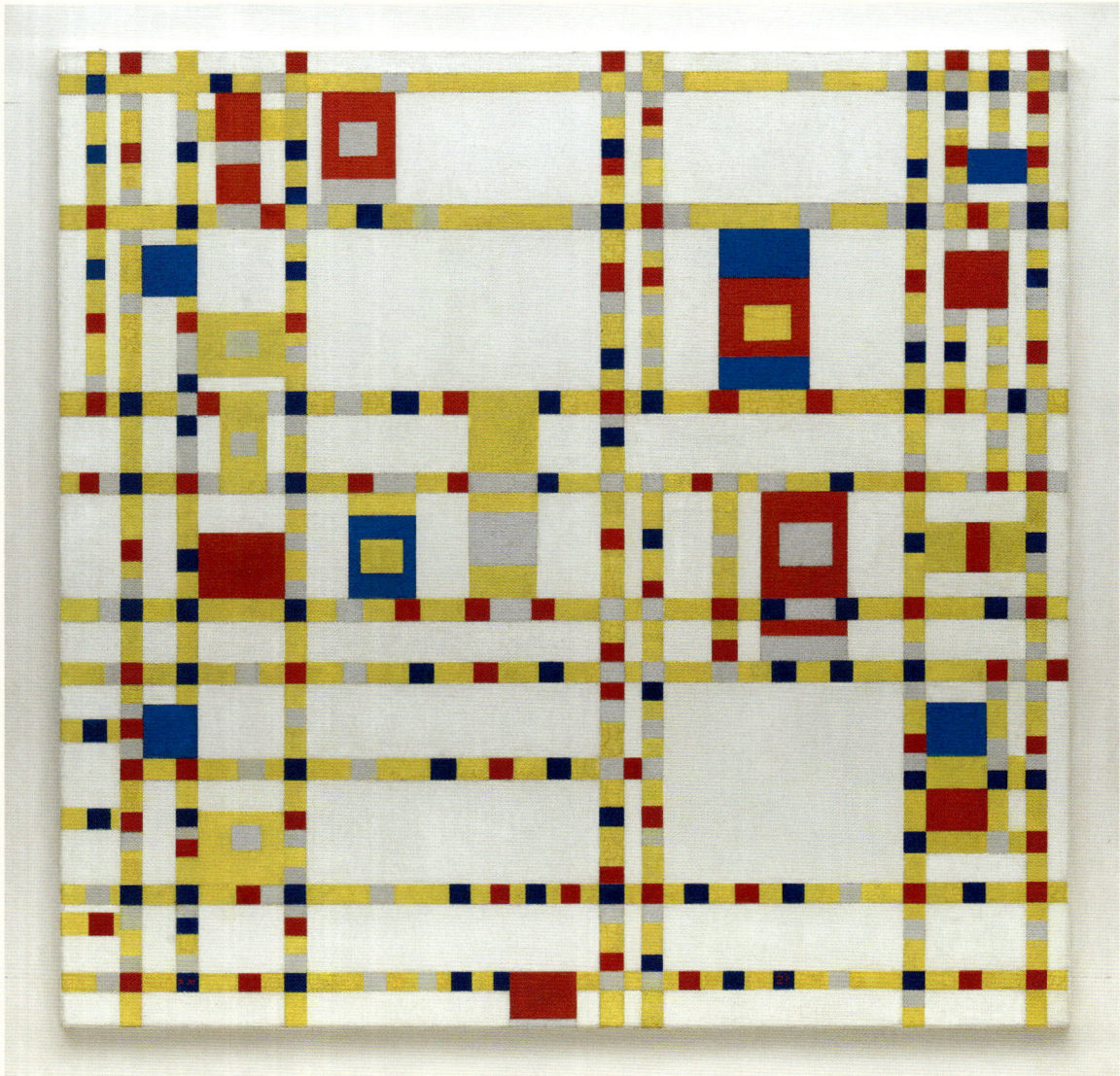

Piet Mondrian

Broadway Boogie Woogie (1942–3)
127 cm x 127 cm
Neoplasticism

If your eyes dance around this painting, then perhaps you're feeling the rhythm of the music that inspired Piet Mondrian when he created it – it is called Boogie Woogie after all! Originally from the Netherlands, the Dutch artist moved to New York City, USA, in early 1940, and fell in love with the city's energy and vibrancy. This painting represents everything that was important to Mondrian, such as the way he made his paintings like grids, with simple vertical and horizontal lines, criss-crossing at different points that feel like the gridded streets of New York itself. It also shows his limited colour palette of red, white, blue, grey, yellow and black, and the brilliance that he achieved by placing one colour next to another. Mondrian liked to play with colours. Can you feel how joyful the artist felt when he made this?

Some artists really want us to first look at only certain parts of an image, because seeing the bigger picture can be easier and more enjoyable if we have taken the time to closely examine the smaller sections. Is there a section that you like the best in this painting?

Could you imagine your own neighbourhood from above, as if making a map? If you choose five or six colours and some simple lines to represent your local streets, could you create your own work of art like Mondrian? Try placing different colours together. Do they make you feel excited, happy or sad?

Frida Kahlo

Self-Portrait with Monkeys (1943)
40.6 cm x 30.5 cm
Self-Portrait

Mexican painter Frida Kahlo is loved and respected all around the world, thanks to her self-portraits. The lifelike, accurate paintings of her face show how she was feeling at the time she painted each one. Her works document her joys and sadnesses, even when battling with illness or struggling with her day-to-day life.

As well as doing self-portraits, Frida frequently chose to paint her pet monkeys, and in this painting each monkey has a strong personality. Two of them are giving Frida loving hugs, and two are playing in the surrounding leaves. Frida looks happy in this painting.

Have you ever tried painting a picture of your own face? See if you can copy a photo of yourself or try looking into a mirror and drawing what you see when you stare straight into the mirror. You could add a pet – even an imaginary one. Is there an animal you'd love to include? Why are you drawn to that animal? Perhaps there's an object from your house you could also include – something that means a lot to you.

Do you know a strong woman like Frida in your own life? Maybe you could draw or paint a portrait of them as a thank-you for how much they've made your life better. It could be one of your teachers, a parent or even one of your friends!

David Hockney

A Bigger Splash (1967)
242.5 cm x 243.9 cm
Pop Art

David Hockney is a very famous British artist, who over the years has painted and drawn many pools and splashes of water, as well as other subjects. A splash happens very quickly, but it took David Hockney two weeks to perfect this splash painting. He liked the idea of taking something that in real life happens in milliseconds, and recreating it in art, slowly and painstakingly. Hockney painted this scene in California, USA, in 1967. He wanted it to capture how hot and humid the city was. Do you think he did?

In the painting, there are no people – not even whoever jumped into the cool water. Who do you think that was? And why did Hockney not paint them – only their splash? Perhaps it was one of Hockney's friends, his family or even the artist himself. Maybe it was one of his two pet sausage dogs, Stanley or Boodgie.

What other things that happen in a split-second could be captured in a painting? A sneeze? Blowing out a candle? Kicking a ball? Hockney sometimes uses his tablet to make new paintings and drawings. Have you ever painted using a tablet or computer?

Roy Lichtenstein

Whaam! (1963)
172.7 cm x 406.4 cm
Pop Art

American artist Roy Lichtenstein was inspired by popular culture, or, more specifically, the illustrations he saw in comic books. Lichtenstein would adopt images from his favourite comics, but he would draw and paint them as giant pieces of art, much much larger than the originals. He would select one small part of a comic book story to emphasise and highlight that single moment. By doing this, he transformed the original image into something new – and created a story in his own, unique style.

A lot of artists find inspiration in art that already exists and will borrow from other artists. Some artists whose work has been used in this way feel sad or angry, but others view it as a compliment and are happy to see their original idea presented in a new way. How would you feel if someone took your work and changed it slightly to make it their own?

Lichtenstein loved to pick out all the small details in the original images as he enlarged them, such as the colourful dots which make up his favourite comic book images. Can you choose a single image from a comic book and draw or paint it much bigger? Could you make a drawing or a painting only using colourful dots? What would you write in a speech bubble?

Hokusai

Under the Wave off Kanagawa (1831)
25.7 cm x 37.9 cm
Ukiyo-e

The artist Katsushika Hokusai was born in Japan in 1760 and is said to have started painting when he was six years old. His most famous work is of a huge blue wave that's about to crash down upon three wooden boats, with Mount Fuji, the famous snow-capped mountain of Japan, shown in the background. It's called *Under the Wave off Kanagawa*, and just by looking at it we can almost feel what it would be like to be underneath this vast body of water! What do you think the people in the three wooden boats are feeling? Are they scared or excited in this moment? What do you think will happen to them and their boats once the wave crashes down?

Hokusai made this work using a famous Japanese wooden block printing technique called ukiyo-e. This involved carving the image into a wooden block and then painting different colour inks onto the wood. He would then turn the wood block over and push it down onto paper to print his image.

You can do something similar with a potato! Cut a potato in half, then carve a shape into the flat side, apply paint onto the image carving and push the potato image onto a piece of paper to see what happens!

Banksy

Girl with Balloon (2002)
Street Art

Banksy is a 'street artist', which means the streets themselves are his canvas. Because of this, his works can appear anywhere and at any time! No one knows who Banksy is, or even if 'Banksy' is his real name, but his graffiti stencils in public areas are seen and talked about all over the world. Using art to say something about the state of the world can sometimes be very powerful, and Banksy uses his images to really make people think. Banksy's work is political – he tells us in just one image what he thinks might be wrong in the world. His artworks are sometimes playful and sometimes very funny, but they are more than just black-and-white images – they are meant to provoke reactions and encourage us to change.

Many people like to create art on public walls, because it can feel like there are no rules and that these are free spaces for everyone to use. But this causes problems, as many walls are not meant to be drawn on – in fact, most are private property and drawing on them would be illegal.

If you were a street artist, what name would you give yourself? What sort of art would you create? To make art like Banksy, create a stencil of an image and use paint to bring it to life. This style makes the outlines of the image very clear so it can be seen clearly from far away.

Bridget Riley

To a Summer's Day 2 (1980) © Bridget Riley 2025. All rights reserved.
115.5 cm x 281 cm
Acrylic on linen
Optical Art/Op Art

British artist Bridget Riley first became well known in the UK in the early 1960s, thanks to her use of black-and-white geometric patterns to create abstract paintings. Her work was part of the Op Art movement, which took its name from the optical illusions created by the paintings themselves – because their shapes and forms could make your eyes see new things, such as vibrations, movement and energy.

Bridget's paintings are always changing, and she has strived to constantly do something new with colour. *To a Summer's Day 2* is a prime example of her work. Even though in its simplest form this is an abstract painting, made up of a series of wavy lines in violet, pink, orange and blue, it still evokes a feeling of a summer breeze. The artist herself has even credited the poetry of Shakespeare as her inspiration.

This work also reminds us of water rippling, as if we were walking along a river or the sea. Isn't it magical that a group of wavy lines can make us think about nature because they somehow seem alive? We even love how the painting makes our eyes go a bit fuzzy as they move over the picture plane! What does her work make you feel? What inspires you? If you could paint anything in nature, what would it be?

Vincent van Gogh

Sunflowers (1888)
92.2 cm x 73 cm
Still Life

Although he is now one of the most famous artists to have ever lived, Vincent van Gogh was practically unknown as an artist until the very last year of his life – and so he sold hardly any paintings at all! He was an obsessive painter who thought about little but his art, and his favourite subject to paint was a 'still life'.

A still life is a painting or a drawing that doesn't have a person in it, but instead uses every day, natural items like fruit or flowers, as well as household objects like chairs, tables and beds. These were all things that Vincent liked to paint. One of his most famous paintings is one that he painted in 1888 showing a vase holding fourteen sunflowers.

As well as painting still life, Vincent also painted people. He created more than forty-three self-portraits in his lifetime, partly because he always wanted to work but didn't always have models to paint, so he would make paintings of himself.

Vincent's brother Theo was his best friend, and they wrote hundreds of letters to each other over their lifetimes. Many of Vincent's letters were full of his artistic ideas and struggles, which is how we know so much about how the artist lived his life. Vincent liked to include little drawings and watercolours with his letters to Theo.

Why don't you try drawing something that you've seen today in your home? It could be something you've eaten, like a piece of fruit. Or something you've used, like a bowl or a spoon.

Romero Britto

Britto Garden (2000)
66 cm x 91.4 cm
Neo-Pop Art

Brazilian-born Romero Britto travelled to Europe to study art when he was twenty, and his life totally changed once he saw how other visual artists were making work. He paints and makes sculptures, combining cartoon images with graffiti. He loves to use bold and vibrant colours to express himself, and he says his work is an expression of hope, happiness, fun and dreams. His joyful and positive artworks have become hugely popular all over the world.

As well as being an artist, Britto is also an activist who has raised money for more than 250 charities and organisations worldwide for causes such as education for children, which is so important.

Look at the black outlines and colourful patterns in the artwork shown here. How does this work make you feel? Try making a picture of your pet or favourite animal using similar techniques. What images would you include and why?

Joan Miró

The Harlequin's Carnival (1924–5)
66 cm x 93 cm
Abstract

Born in the city of Barcelona, Spain, Joan Miró started drawing at around seven years old. As a teenager, he went to business school and also took art classes but soon decided to study art full time. Miró had moments of deep sadness throughout his lifetime, but said that painting helped ease these moments and made him feel calm. He would paint his early childhood memories and mix them with what was happening around him as an adult, and also with what he was dreaming about.

Miró loved colour, as well as thinking about the vastness of the universe at night. In his paintings we can see shooting stars, planets and constellations. Can you see other shapes in his paintings?

Can you remember your dreams? Have you ever tried drawing or painting them? What do you think is Miró's favourite colour? You could even try painting what you see at night, using bright colours like Miró.

Giuseppe Arcimboldo

Vertumnus (1591)
70 cm x 58 cm
Mannerism

Have you ever made funny faces with your food? Fried eggs for eyes, a sausage for a mouth and baked beans for hair? Well, Giuseppe Arcimboldo was doing this with his paintings over 500 years ago! Born in Milan, Italy, Giuseppe began his career as a designer of stained glass, before moving his craft on to painting fantastical looking faces and heads made up of fruits and vegetables, flowers, books and even fish. Giuseppe's style of art was part of the Mannerism movement which developed during the 16th century. Mannerist art is easy to identify thanks to its over-the-top focus on artificiality and sensuality, as well as distorting the human figure. Mannerist artists were inspired by Renaissance masters (such as Raphael and Michaelangelo) but took their creativity to an even more exaggerated artifice and often used bold, unnatural colours too.

Can you spot all the foods Giuseppe painted while creating *Vertumnus*? What items could you use today to make a portrait of your family or friends? Giuseppe used a lot of flowers and green plants to make the clothing in his portraits. Could you design a sweatshirt out of grass and leaves? His paintings are meant to make us smile and laugh – do you think they are funny? Try painting different fruits and vegetables – like a banana and some cherries, an apple and maybe some grapes – then, cut them out and make them into a collage to create a face.

Diego Rivera

Dream of a Sunday Afternoon in Alameda Park (1947)
15.6 m x 4.7 m
Mural

Diego Rivera first started drawing on the walls of his childhood home in Mexico at the age of three, so his parents placed canvases and chalkboards on their walls to encourage his creativity. When he was ten, he chose to study art and went to an art academy in Mexico City before moving to Paris, France, when he was old enough. He became famous for painting very large fresco murals all around the world – especially in his home country of Mexico and in the USA. Diego's murals are filled with people who are closely packed together, many dressed in traditional Mexican clothing.

Fresco murals are pictures painted directly onto a wall, much like Diego did as a child – but, with frescoes, the paint is dry and the walls are wet! As the wet plaster on the walls dries, it sucks in the dry paint and sets it. This technique has been used by artists all over the world for centuries, and some frescoes are thousands of years old.

Why do you think these paintings have survived for so long? Have you ever tried drawing or painting directly onto a wall? Make sure you get permission before attempting it!

Jim Dine

Four Hearts (1969)
32.4 cm x 31.8 cm

As a child, Jim Dine lived with his grandfather, who was the owner of a hardware store in Cincinnati, USA. Jim remembers seeing the saws and drills, hammers and screwdrivers, nails and bolts that were sold in the store – all of which he felt were magical. These objects became important motifs in his artwork. A motif is a particular image that appears many times in an artist's work, throughout their career.

Hearts have also been a huge motif for Jim Dine, as has the cartoon character Pinocchio, which he watched as a movie with his mother when he was six years old. Artists sometimes use the same image over and over again because they want to understand why they love it so much. By repeating it, they can learn more about it every time.

Do you have a favourite motif? Maybe you like drawing hearts just like Jim Dine, or maybe flowers? Find a motif that you like, and try making different artworks with it. You could draw your motif, paint it, mould it in clay, or use an iPad to animate it. Find an image you are fascinated by and explore all the ways it can be made into an artwork.

Alexander Calder

Red Maze III (1954)
142.2 cm x 182.9 cm
Sculpture

Alexander Calder's parents were both artists, and they encouraged him to create from a young age. In time, his love for art became too strong to ignore, and Calder did become an artist. However, instead of doing straightforward artworks, Calder started making sculptures that moved! He made his first artworks with wire – a thin, bendable metal that challenged the traditional idea of sculpture as a solid mass. Critics described these wire sculptures as 'drawing in space' because he would use the wire itself to create a drawing in mid-air. He also created a whole miniature circus that he carried around in large suitcases and performed all over the world!

In time, Calder made bigger works, like the one you can see in the picture, from sheets of metal that hung on wires and moved around when lightly touched, or if a breeze hit them. He called these 'mobiles'.

Gwen John

The Convalescent
(1918–19)
33.7 cm x 25.4 cm
History Painting

When Gwen John was alive, from 1876 until 1939, the world saw women very differently to how they do now. Men who were artists were seen as important, whereas women artists did not get the same recognition – thankfully, that has changed. Gwen painted self-portraits, as well as portraits of many other women she met and became friends with. She described her style as painting in 'blobs', because she would apply paint in small mounds all over the canvas, and then push and pull it together with a brush to make her images come alive, just like in the picture above.

Gwen's older brother Augustus was also an artist – and he was famous for his work during his lifetime. At the time Gwen wasn't well known, yet today more people enjoy her work. Why do you think this is?

Have you ever tried painting in blobs like Gwen John? Cover a canvas in little dabs of wet paint, like a mosaic, and then see if you can make a picture form by connecting them all with a brush. Look at the clothes of the woman in Gwen's painting – it's brilliant to see the way that people dressed over one hundred years ago. Do you think in another hundred years people will think that our clothes are very different to theirs?

Alberto Giacometti

Walking Man I (1960)
183 cm x 25.5 cm x 95 cm
Sculpture

Alberto Giacometti was born in Switzerland. His father was a painter, and Alberto grew up surrounded by his father's work. So, when as a teenager he also started to make paintings, drawings and sculptures, it felt natural for him. Alberto's work was very lifelike at first, but later that changed.

When Alberto was in his late thirties, the Second World War broke out. This was a very frightening time for many people, and Alberto was greatly affected by what he saw and what he read about in newspapers. He started to make tall, stretched out figures from clay, plaster and paint. They felt fragile and at times almost like skeletons. He used hard materials like bronze, which meant the figures were strong, but still appeared vulnerable. Alberto liked to use people he loved as models, including his brother, parents and wife. They would sit or stand in front of him for hours and even days while he painted and moulded them out of clay.

Have you ever tried to make an artwork of somebody you love? Perhaps by painting, drawing or moulding their figure from plasticine? How do you think they would feel having to sit still for a long time while you made your artwork of them? What if they needed to scratch their face or use the toilet – could you use your memory to continue making them, as sometimes Alberto had to do?

Alberto loved the human head, and he made lots and lots of sculptures of different heads. What is your favourite body part? Could you make a sculpture of it? A clay foot? Maybe an arm stretched out of plasticine, or a pair of painted eyes? Look at the people you love, pay attention to what you like most about them and make art from that feature.

Henri Rousseau

Tiger in a Tropical Storm/Surprised! (1891)
129.8 cm x 161.9 cm
Post-Impressionism

French artist Henri Rousseau was born in 1844, and when he grew up his main job was being a tax collector. For him, painting was just a hobby, which he didn't start doing until he was in his thirties. Henri painted jungle scenes over and over again, even though he had never left his home country of France. Filled with exotic animals, like monkeys and tigers, as well as beautiful flowers, green plants and vines twisting around tall trees, Henri's paintings feel like an escape from his day job.

This painting has two titles, *Tiger in a Tropical Storm* and *Surprised!*. Why do you think the artist needed two titles for the work? Do you think the tiger seems surprised, or scared? What can you see that may have scared the tiger – is it the rain from the storm, or the wind bending the trees, or maybe the lightning flashing in the night sky? What else can you see in the image, and what does the tiger look like it's about to do? The tiger is looking at something beyond the canvas, what do you think this could be?

When the artist was alive, many people didn't like his work as they thought it was too simple, yet, in time, Henri Rousseau's art has become increasingly important. Do you like his painting style? Notice how all the plants are green, but they are all different shades of green. Try painting a plant yourself but use different shades of the same colour to make the image.

Frank Bowling is a painter known for his abstract, colourful works. His paintings often refer to his life and family – including moving from Bartica, Guyana, to London, UK, in 1953. Maps, architecture and geometry all play a big part in his work too, along with bright, vibrant colours and textures which he creates from acrylic gel and foam, as well as from more traditional types of paint and pigment. Bowling is known for adding 'found materials' to the surface of his work, including paint pot lids, paint brushes and bits of leftover canvas or fabric.

Many of Bowling's works tend to be on a large scale – and some of his paintings are absolutely giant, such as the one shown here which is almost 5 metres long! It's easy to get lost in the beautiful colours, patterns and marks on the surface of each painting. The unique way that Bowling creates his art – by staining the surface of a canvas, stitching canvases together, or even pouring paint directly from the pot onto the surface – alongside his bold colour selections, has led to worldwide recognition.

Frank Bowling

Dog Daze (1971)
273.6 cm x 492 cm
Abstract

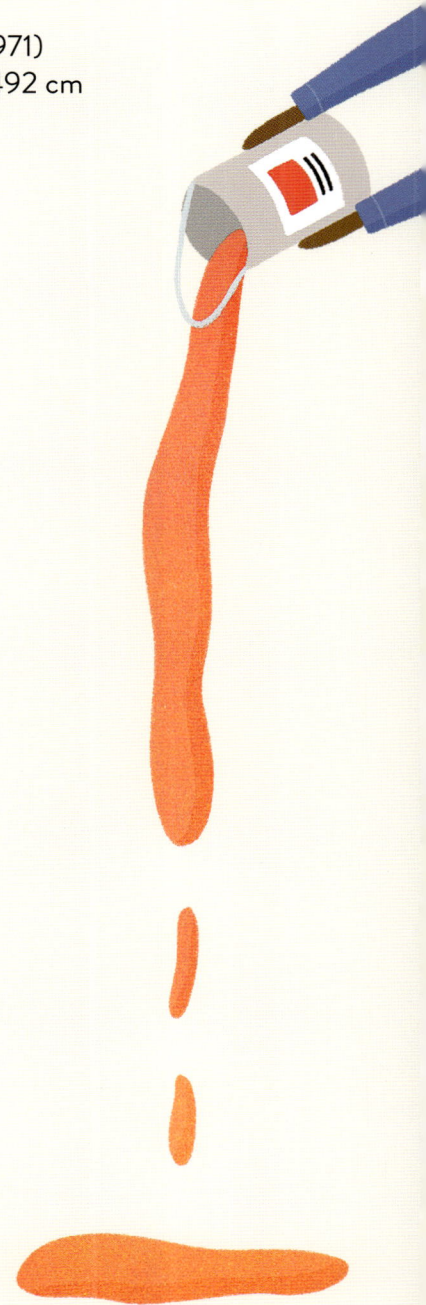

Frank Bowling has achieved a lot during his life, including being the first ever Black male artist to become a Royal Academician at the Royal Academy, which is a very prestigious award, as well as a knighthood from Queen Elizabeth II in 2020. He is one of Britain's most famous abstract painters. Abstract art is created using shapes, colour and gestural mark making to create an image.

Would you like to try making an abstract painting? Why not begin by using a wash of one colour in the background, and then add another colour on top. You could try to use different types of brush strokes but also different shapes. Maybe think of geometry to paint different shapes alongside each other. Try to paint an emotion, by making marks that express how you feel on the inside. It could be a joyous feeling, a funny feeling or even frustration or confusion. Painting your feelings in an abstract way can be really useful and exciting!

Hilma af Klint

No. 1, Altarpiece (Altarbild) (1915)
237.5 cm x 179.5 cm
Abstract

Hilma af Klint was a talented Swedish painter best known for her abstract art. Abstract art does not try to represent actual objects, landscapes or people, but instead focuses solely on mark making, lines or shapes, and a wide variety of colours to create the final artwork. Hilma is celebrated for a system she devised in which she included messages and signs within her paintings. Colours would take on special meanings: for example, yellow represents femininity, blue represents masculinity and green represents harmony.

There are many layers and stories to discover within Hilma's work – the more you look the more you can see, or at least imagine. The shapes she used are also significant as they all have different meanings, and, at the time she made *Altarpiece No. 1*, that was still a very new idea. In fact, Hilma is thought to be one of the first ever abstract painters. This makes her a pioneer – just like many other women artists, such as Frida Kahlo and Georgia O'Keefe – and her work continues to inspire people today.

We love this legacy and how, within her paintings, she allows us to explore and uncover symbols and secrets lying deep within the art itself. What are some of your favourite shapes? Can you overlap them in a drawing and see what other shapes you could create?

Georgia O'Keeffe

Jimson Weed/White Flower No. 1 (1932)
121.9 cm x 101.6 cm
Modernism

Georgia O'Keefe was born in Wisconsin, USA, in 1887, and decided she wanted to be an artist at the age of twelve... yes, twelve! Her best-known paintings are of nature – these include the desert in New Mexico where she spent her later life, animal skulls and bones she found whilst walking in this desert, as well as the insides of flowers, such as poppies and the white flower in this painting.

The main thing that made O'Keeffe's work unique was how her paintings didn't just accurately depict flowers, but instead expressed how each flower made her feel. She would connect her own emotions with the subject in front of her, and pour those emotions into each painting. We hope you'll agree that her art is beautiful, atmospheric and energised because of this passion and intensity. Georgia carefully chose her colour palette too, and this helped reveal her emotional state on each canvas.

We love how she combines two styles of art – Realism and Abstraction– into a unique visual language of her own creation. She's so popular that one of her paintings – the one we've included here – sold for US$44 million in 2014. At the time, that was the highest price ever paid for a painting by a female artist in an auction. Georgia O'Keeffe is an inspiring record breaker!

Do you have a favourite flower? Can you find a flower outside in your garden or local park? Why not try making your own painting of the inside of that flower!

Robert Indiana

LOVE (1981)
243.8 cm x 243.8 cm x 121.9 cm
Sculpture, Pop Art

Robert Indiana was born in 1928 and grew up to become one of America's most famous artists. In the 1960s, Robert played a key role in developing painting for the new Pop Art generation, and in particular for his love of assemblage art using found materials like scrap wood and metal to create his sculptures. He was also one of the leading artists to use language, words and even numbers as a central part of his art.

One of our favourite ever sculptures is of a word: LOVE. We love how this sculpture has captured the imagination of people all around the globe. It's even been translated into other languages, such as AMOR in Spanish. This work has been installed in all kinds of public places, and is a joyous public artwork to encounter. It's so popular that it's been reproduced as fridge magnets, T-shirts and postcards, and is sold in museums worldwide. Perhaps what is so good about it is its directness and clarity. It's a very simple idea, but sometimes the simple ideas are the most powerful!

Did you know that words or poems can be art? We love how surprising and impactful this artwork was when it was first made, and how it continues to surprise people today. It is bold and clear, and now iconic! Did you notice the layout of the four letters? Which one is slightly different to the rest? That's right, the 'O' is in italics, so it's slanting to the right. This choice is very clever as it keeps the viewer interested. Indiana's sculpture is a lasting example of the power of Pop Art and its often positive messages.

Do you have something positive to say in your artwork? If you could share a happy message with the world, what would you say?

Augusta Savage

The Harp (1939)
27.3 cm x 24.1 cm x 10.2 cm
Sculpture

Augusta Savage was an innovative sculptor from Florida, USA, who conveyed powerful messages through her work. She was born in 1892 and dedicated her adult life to not only making art, but to the fight against racism. She was a key figure within the Harlem Renaissance, which was a 1920s arts movement that celebrated African American art, music, literature and dance. This movement was very important because it brought Black artistic and cultural history to the attention of the wider public.

Savage influenced and taught many artists, and her art continues to inspire many more today. She founded an art school and studio spaces for Black artists – in particular, for other Black female artists, who she would encourage and whose artwork she would exhibit.

sing
and
voice
every
Lift

As a child, Savage made sculptures out of local clay in Florida, and she continued to explore sculpture throughout her life, largely in plaster. Her most famous work, *The Harp*, was a large-scale, painted plaster sculpture that was nearly 5 metres tall! It was commissioned for the 1939 New York World's Fair, and was inspired by the Black National Anthem, 'Lift Every Voice and Sing'. The sculpture depicted a choir singing, and aimed to reflect community, strength and liberation. After the fair closed, the sculpture was destroyed because the money couldn't be raised to turn it into a permanent bronze. But smaller versions were cast in bronze, and a number of these have lasted and become a tribute to celebrate African American contributions to music and art.

What causes are you most passionate about? Try and design a piece of art that speaks to that cause – perhaps it's a slogan, or a drawing, a sculpture or even a poem.

Jordan Casteel

Barbershop (2015)
182.9 cm x 137.2 cm
Figurative

Jordan Casteel was born in Denver, Colorado, USA, and spent time living in Harlem, New York City. She loved the Harlem community and would ask many of the people she met there if she could take pictures of them so that she could create paintings from the photographs. Many of the people Jordan painted had never had their portrait painted before, and some of these paintings have ended up in major museum collections and on gallery walls. This is very important for Jordan who, as an African American, rarely saw anybody that looked like her when she visited galleries and museums as a child. Through her work, and the work of many other artists of colour, more people from younger generations can now see themselves in art.

Have you seen anyone who looks like you in a photograph or painting in a museum or art book? Who would you like to see represented in art more often?

To create art like Jordan Casteel, you could first try taking photos of people you like – but ask their permission first. Then use the photos for reference as you paint or draw them.

Artists work every single day to make their art better and better, and we describe an art career as 'an art practice'. For many artists, practice makes perfect. Would you like an art practice like Jordan Casteel? Do you think you could and would like to make art every day?

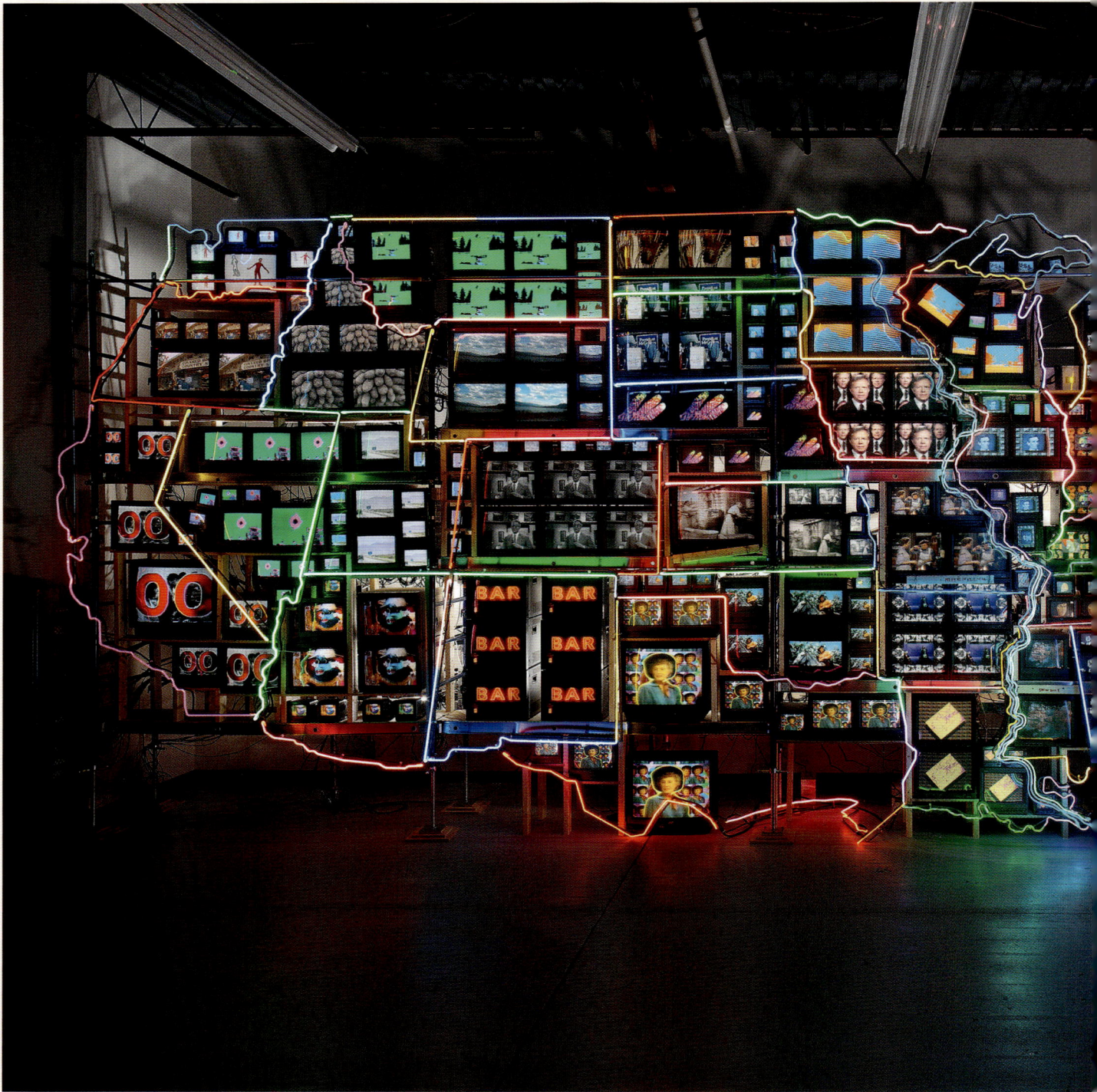

Nam June Paik

Electronic Superhighway: Continental U.S., Alaska, Hawaii (1995)
4.6 m x 1.2 m x 12 m
Video Art

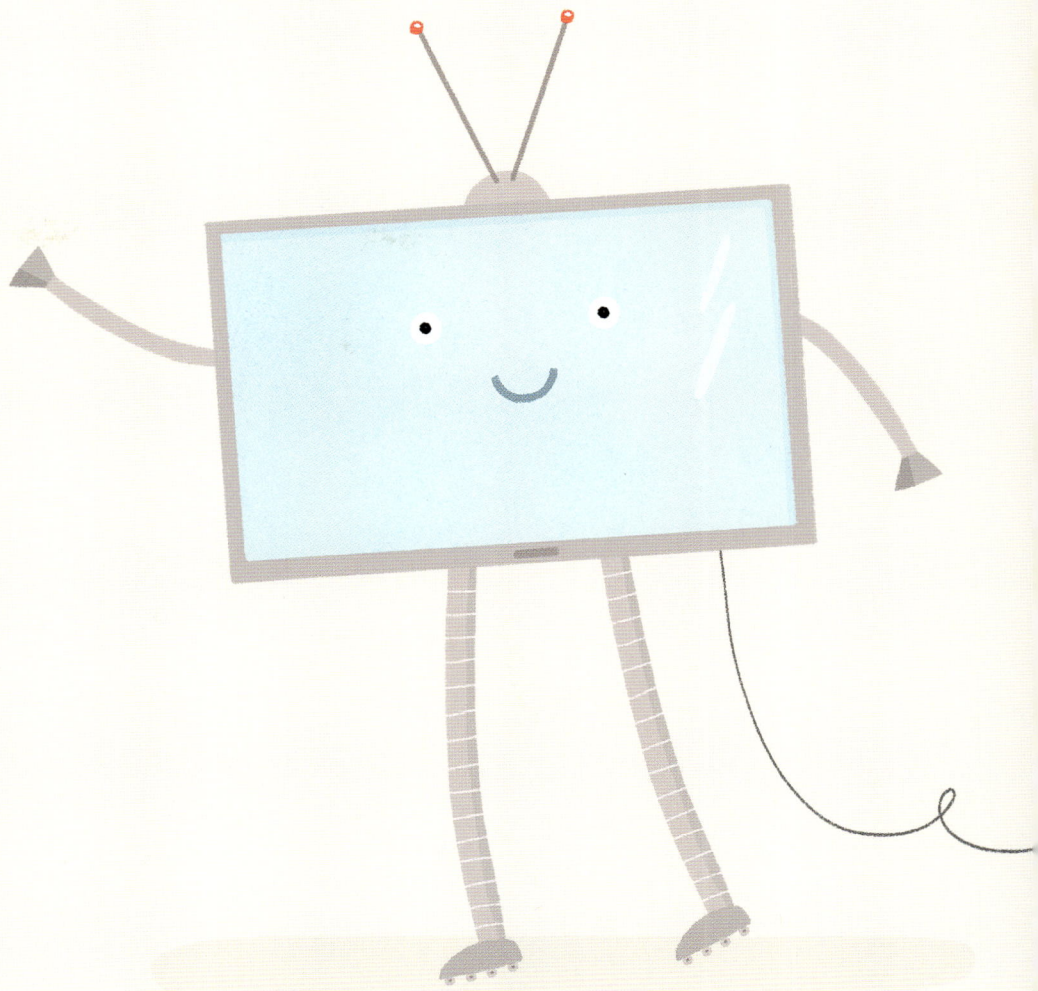

Nam June Paik was a Korean artist who became famous for using sculpture and videos together. His sculptures of life-size robots made out of video screens, toys and old radios were very popular. He also made videos to reflect the personality of each of his robots, and would play them on the TV screens. Nam June Paik played with gender, using curved screens for his female robots and more angular screens for the male ones. He made these in the early 1980s, when technologies such as tape recorders, video games and video recording devices were starting to be used by human beings on a daily basis. Nam June Paik found this cultural shift interesting and, through his art, questioned what the future might be like for us all.

Do you think he got it right? Would you like a robot made out of video screens in your house? If you had to make a short film that would play in one of the robot TV screens, what would it show? If you're able to find an old radio, ask an adult to help you to carefully take it apart, and then try making a robot sculpture out of the pieces. It could be a human-like figure, or an animal, a vehicle or something totally new.

Lee Ufan is a South Korean minimalist painter and sculptor. A minimalist artist uses very simple lines and basic forms to make art, often wanting the audience to make up their own mind about what the work might represent. Using a large white surface, Lee Ufan mixes oil with paint pigment and creates his paintings with just one or two colours. They can vary in style, ranging from small beaker-like shapes, to long lines going up and down the canvas – almost like arrows or rockets.

What do you feel when you see Lee's work? Many people think that this type of art is very simple, but it takes artists like Lee many years to create something so simple and yet absolutely precise. Have a go at drawing your own simplistic piece and see what it makes you feel like.

Lee Ufan

From Line (1978)
181.8 cm x 227.5 cm
Minimalism

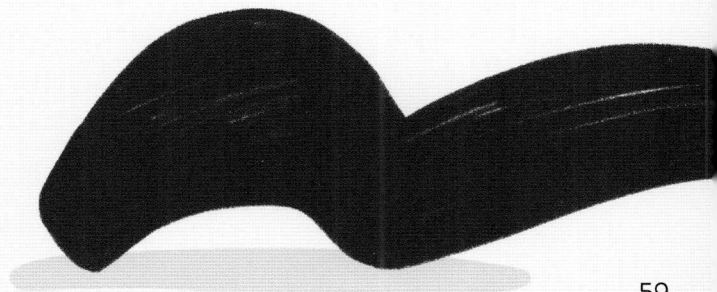

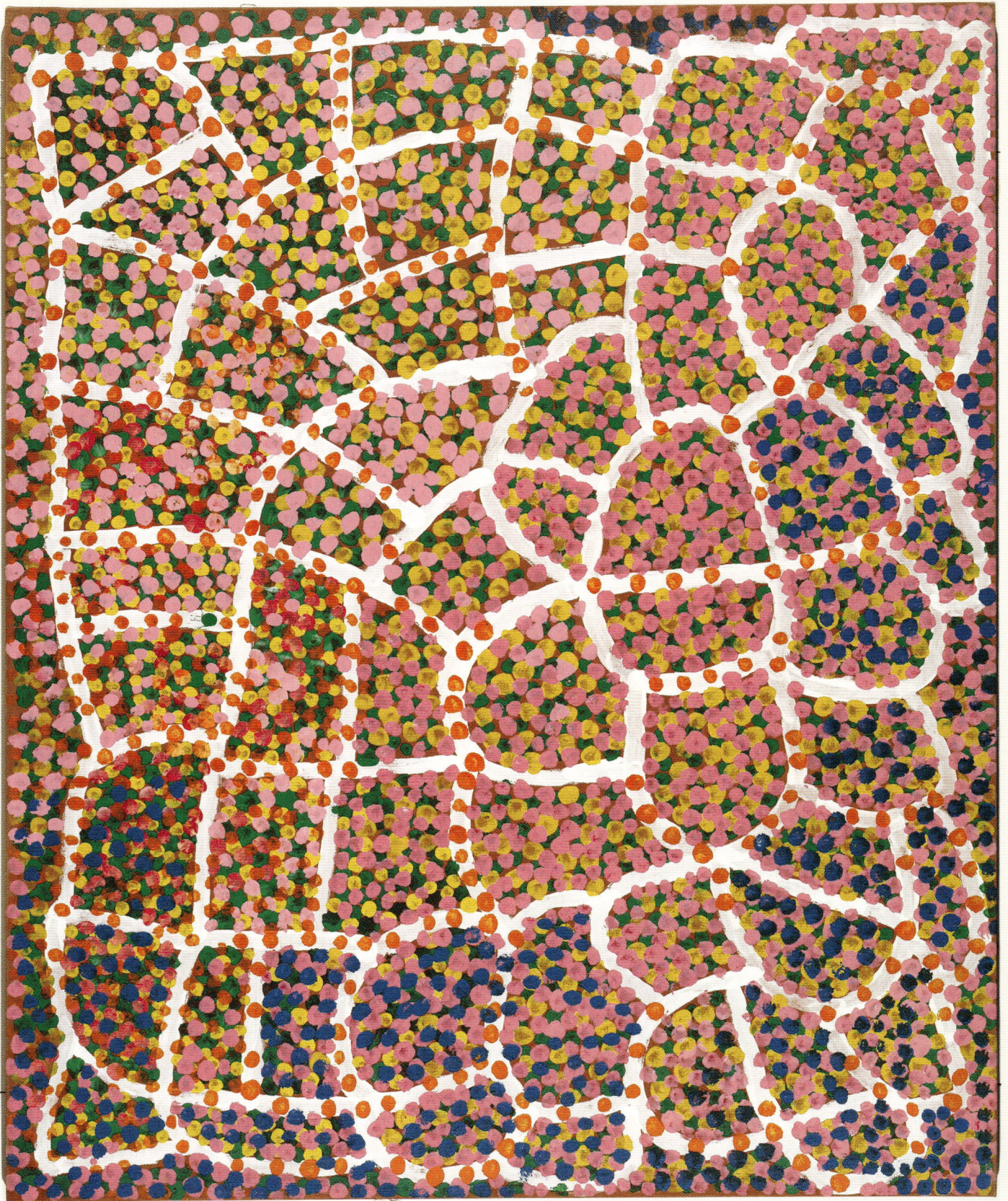

Emily Kam Kngwarray

Awelye (1991)
152.2 cm x 121.8 cm
Abstract

Emily Kam Kngwarray didn't start painting until she was in her seventies, yet she produced over 3,000 paintings before she died eight years later. This means she created around one painting each day! She was an Aboriginal Australian, and continues to be one of the most important and successful artists in Australian history. Emily painted on large canvases by placing them on the ground and sitting cross-legged on top of them. She would use a very long brush to reach all the areas of the canvas.

Have you tried sitting on the floor while you paint? If you get a large sheet of paper and the longest brush you can find, try to sit cross-legged while you paint, just like Emily. Remember to use big brush strokes and bright colours, such as reds and yellows.

Antony Gormley

Lost Horizon I (2008)
Installation view, Royal Academy of Arts, London (2019)
Contemporary Art

Antony Gormley is a world-famous sculptor who makes huge sculptures out of very heavy metal, and also tiny sculptures out of clay and wire. He uses the human figure to imagine artistic ideas, and the closest human figure to him is himself. So, he moulds himself out of plaster, or scans himself and uses the computer to create an image of what the finished sculpture should look like – and how big or small it should be – before making it. However, even though he is known as a sculptor, Antony says that drawing is his most important daily activity – in fact, he says, 'A day without drawing is a day lost.'

Could you draw every day? It might be a small doodle while talking to friends, or a big and colourful sketch that you really have to think about – but try drawing something (anything that you can think of!) every single day for one month and see how you feel.

Antony installs his sculptures in public areas, like beaches and buildings, or along the sides of motorways and even in rivers and the sea. He does this because when an artwork is in areas used every day by the public, lots and lots of people get to see it – many more than if it were in a gallery. He is called a 'public artist'. If you were to make a work of art for the public, what would it be – and where would you like to put it?

Jean-Michel Basquiat

Grillo (1984)
243.8 cm x 537.2 cm x 47 cm
Neo-Expressionism
© Estate of Jean-Michel Basquiat. Licensed by Artestar, New York.

Jean-Michel Basquiat was born in Brooklyn, New York, USA in 1960, and has won hearts around the world for his passionate paintings. Encouraged by his Puerto Rican mother Mathilde to visit art galleries from a young age, Jean-Michel became a keen artist, and especially loved drawing cartoons. His father was from Haiti and was a big jazz music fan, so music was also a big influence!

As a teenager Jean-Michel moved to a school in New York City, where he fell in love with graffiti art and began painting on street walls and empty buildings under the nickname SAMO. His street drawings got a lot of attention, so eventually he began to paint on a more traditional, permanent surface – canvas – and his paintings became part of a new generation of artist called the Neo-Expressionists.

Jean-Michel's paintings have lots of energy, bringing together words (he could speak English, Spanish and French), signs, symbols, figures and drawings of the human body, along with splashes of bright colour. He also included graffiti in his paintings!

Sadly, in 1988, Jean-Michel died at the age of 27. Thanks to his love of art, he made more than 600 paintings in his lifetime, and well over a thousand drawings. We love Jean-Michel's work because he made art about the big issues that mattered deeply to him, including wealth, poverty and the fight against racism and injustice.

Try drawing while listening to music – perhaps music from the 1980s! Start by drawing ten symbols onto a piece of paper. The symbols could be anything that comes into your mind, or maybe even something from a song lyric. Try drawing different shapes, like a circle, triangle or even a dinosaur or cartoon character. You could even draw a crown. See how many symbols and figures you can think of!

Yayoi Kusama

Pumpkin (2013)
260 cm x 245 cm
Pumpkin (2013)
210 cm x 205 cm
Pumpkin (2013)
130 cm x 125 cm
Mixed Media

Yayoi Kusama is a Japanese artist who many call the Queen of Polka Dots! She gained this title because almost all of her artworks feature dots – many, many, many polka dots. Her obsession with dots began as a child when she started to have hallucinations. She recalls, one day, seeing a field of flowers and believing that the flowers were speaking to her. She remembered the flowers had heads. The heads of flowers looked like polka dots and all she could see was dots upon dots in the flower field.

This theme has become so important to Kusama that she has created sculptures, paintings and even entire rooms where she tries to recreate this sensation of seeing dots forever and ever. Her work is very playful and, thanks to the repetition of dots, it's very fun to look at! Her sculptures have included giant pumpkins covered in dots such as the ones shown here. Her art has gone on to be seen as a very important part of Pop Art but also the Minimalist movement.

Would you like to draw something out of polka dots? What about drawing a suit or a dress and covering it in polka dots? Kusama herself loved to create fashion as well as art, and she has often combined the two to great effect. Would you like to design clothes that are covered in polka dots?

Andy Warhol

Marilyn Monroe (1967)
91 cm x 91 cm each
Pop Art

Andy Warhol is the most famous Pop Artist there ever was. His work was inspired by pop culture, and this meant that anything – from a Campbell's tomato soup can to a photo of the actress Marilyn Monroe – could be his subject. He would often use an image over and over again, introducing differences, and then hang the images in a row. For example, he took Marilyn Monroe's face and painted it repeatedly in different colours.

In his early career, Warhol started out as an illustrator, creating drawings and cartoons for magazines. He developed a very strong personal style, and is still remembered for his blonde hair and the many wigs that he chose to wear and photograph himself wearing. He liked the idea of creating a persona – a character that he liked to play.

Some of our favourite artworks by Warhol are of animals, in particular his Endangered Species series, in which he created screen prints of animals that were under threat of becoming extinct, including a lion, frog, rhinoceros, butterfly and monkey.

Warhol was a great collaborator who would invite his artist friends to create paintings with him. For example, he made paintings with other now-famous artists like Jean-Michel Basquiat. Have you ever made an artwork with one of your friends? It can be really fun to come together and share ideas. Maybe you can both bring your own unique style of drawing into one picture. If one of you starts a drawing, can the other one finish it?

Endangered Species (complete set, 1983)
96 cm x 96 cm each
Pop Art

Tracey Emin

I Want My Time With You (2018)
20 m
Autobiographical/Confessional

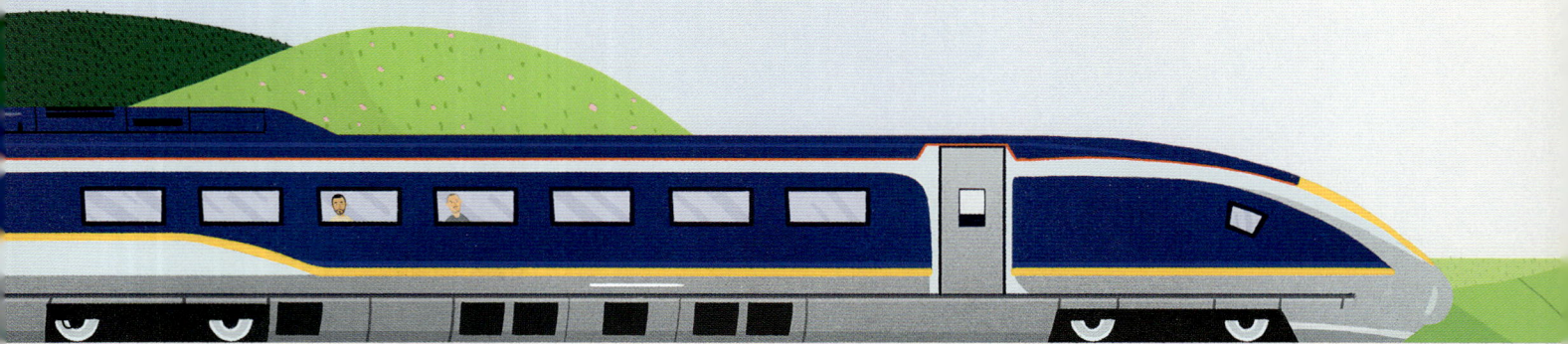

Tracey Emin is a British artist who makes autobiographical work that is very personal. Her art tells stories from her life and conveys how she feels about her relationships with her loved ones. Even her pet cats, Teacup, Pancake and Docket, have featured in her artworks! Her art is very thoughtful and can be deeply touching. It has also brought much happiness to people all around the world.

She is best known for her colourful paintings, giant bronze sculptures and scratchy drawings, but also for her installations that include many of her personal belongings. These installations include hand-sewn applique blankets using fabrics she kept from her childhood, as well as her own bed (yes! her actual bed!), which was nominated for the prestigious Turner Prize award in 1999. Tracey really does help us to experience art in a bold, new way!

Writing and poetry is often at the heart of Tracey's artworks. We really love her massive neon text work installed at St Pancras train station in London. This giant sentence reads, I Want My Time With You, and hangs from the glass ceiling of one of the UK's busiest train stations. Thanks to this popular location, it is free for everyone to view over and over again.

Can you think of a phrase or poem that you would like to see in lights? Try writing about someone you care about. Would you like to create an artwork and share it with the world in a public place? What would you create and where would you install your public artwork? It could be in your town centre or high street, or maybe in your local park? Dream big!

Katherine Bernhardt

Pink (2019)
76 cm x 60 cm
Contemporary Painting

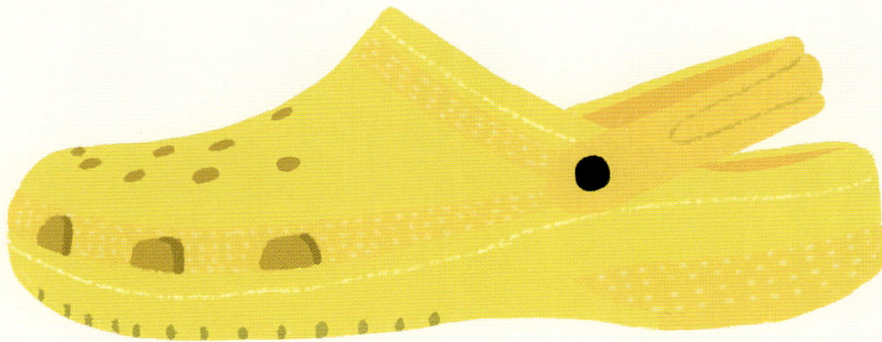

Katherine Bernhardt is a painter who was born in Clayton, Missouri, USA, in 1975 and is now based in St Louis, also in Missouri. She is best known for her hyper-colourful paintings, which include her favourite things from popular culture – from cartoon characters such as the Pink Panther, Garfield, E.T. and Bart Simpson, to sharks, tropical birds and the Cookie Monster. In her paintings, Katherine also likes to include everyday objects from her house, such as toilet rolls, Crocs and Coca-Cola bottles.

What makes Katherine stand out as an artist is the way she paints. She draws the outline of each object or character using spray paint, and then fills in the outline with washy acrylic paint. This means that her paintings have a strong energy and playful sense of joy and fun.

If you were to create your own grid painting, what items would you choose to include? Katherine has even featured bags of Doritos tortilla chips, as well as her toothbrush and toothpaste in her paintings . . . so it really can be ANYTHING in your home. You could start by thinking about the objects you love most.

Cassi Namoda

Little is Enough For Those with Love Mimi Nakupenda (2019)
167.6 cm x 233.7 cm
Autobiographical, Contemporary Painting

Cassi Namoda is a painter who makes very personal works which reflect on cultural myths and history, but also look to her present life and her dreams of the future. She grew up in Maputo, Mozambique and her memories of her childhood home have often been the subject of her atmospheric paintings. Cassi has travelled the world a lot, and during her travels she has made drawings of the landscapes she's visited and the people she's seen – whether it be family and friends, or strangers she's met along the way. Some of the places she has visited include Haiti, the USA, Uganda, Kenya and countries across Europe.

We love the references to music, dancing and nature in Cassi's work. Whether painting sunsets, palm trees or the desert, Cassi often uses bright, bold colours, and some of her works use blocks of colour to create intense emotions. Cassi also likes to tell stories in her paintings.

Can you think of a story you'd like to tell in your art? Try painting a group of people similar to those found in Cassi's art, and think about the relationships between the people. Are they family? Are they friends? How did they meet? What brings them together? Are they at a party or are they getting ready for a dinner?

Ramesh Mario Nithiyendran

Undergods installation (2023)
Sculpture

Ramesh is a Sri Lankan artist who is now based in Sydney, Australia. He's known for his exciting sculptures of monsters which he makes from fired ceramic. Some of his works reference history by taking inspiration from gods, myths and folklore, but they can also be inspired by human rituals, religions and the natural world of animals.

He creates the ceramics using a clay, and then adds a glaze – which is essentially a colourful liquid, a bit like paint. He then puts the clay sculptures into a very hot kiln to heat them up until they become solid sculptures which are very strong.

The main theme in Ramesh's work is a magical world of monsters! He starts out by drawing pictures of monsters in a notepad or on paper, using his imagination to think up wild and wonderful creatures. Can you try to draw a monster? Think of ways to make its body look really colourful, and try to include different patterns or marks.

Have you ever tried to make a sculpture? If you have some plasticine or moulding clay, you could create a monster of your own, similar to Ramesh's. What shape would its head be? Will it have big eyes? Will it be short or tall?

You CAN be an artist too!

Art is something all of us can do! Some people do it for fun, whereas others take it seriously and dedicate a lot of their time to making art. If you really love making art and want to spend all your free time creating it, then maybe it's time to call yourself an artist, just like the inspiring people we've talked about in this book!

Some of the most important things to think about if you want to become an artist are:

- What do you want to say?
- How do you feel?
- What are the things that matter to you?

Your art could be inspired by people, objects, animals or the environment. Or perhaps you want to help others. Art is whatever you want it to be! You have the power and creativity, just remember to practise. The more art you make the more you will improve.

Develop your creativity!

Try different exercises to stretch your creativity. Go for a walk with your family or friends, and while you are walking, look all around you. Pay close attention to everything that surrounds you. What can you see? What can you hear? What do you feel?

Sit on a park bench and draw what you notice, or walk down a street and think about the parts of the street that you like most. You could draw a car on the road, a bicycle, house or street lamp. A lot of what makes you an artist is the ability to look at and absorb the world around you.

A magical world of colours!

Colour can be one of the most important tools for an artist, and there are so many different colours to choose from. Look around you right now – how many colours there are in the objects around you? Does the natural light or electric light change the way the colours look? Try using colouring pencils to re-create the different colours.

This is a useful way to begin making art, but it's important to remember that art doesn't necessarily mean copying what you see in front of you. Sometimes it's fun to break the rules and do things differently! Use your imagination to dream up different colours for the objects around you. TVs don't have to be black, they can be pink! Grass can be blue! The sun can be purple! Have a go at changing the colours of objects and see how fun they can look.

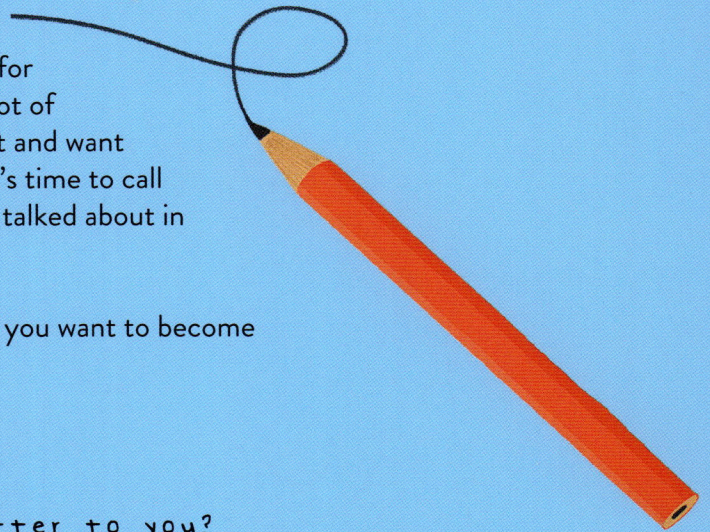

Art techniques!

When it comes to making and creating art, many artists begin by drawing. This is an affordable and easy way to start learning about how the world works, and how you relate to the world around you. Drawing is easy too, because you can take a pencil and paper with you anywhere, and it's easy to move around indoors and outdoors! You can also draw with different types of pencils – like charcoal, which makes a thicker line compared to a regular pencil.

Painting is a natural next step. The three primary colours of red, blue and yellow can be mixed to create secondary and tertiary colours – just mix equal parts of two primary colours to create a secondary colour. Red and blue create purple, red and yellow create orange, and yellow and blue create green. Whatever colour you want to make, you just mix!

Collage is also a popular art form, and many artists create collages by cutting out images from newspapers or magazines. It's really fun to look for images that you feel 'speak' to you and then create new images by collaging and sticking them together in new arrangements. Let your imagination run wild!

Sculpture is another popular medium for making art. Similar to drawing, sculpture begins with your hands. You can mould and sculpt plasticine or clay to create anything you want – maybe start with a sculpture of yourself. It can be time-consuming but really satisfying.

These are just a few ways you can make art. There are famous artists around the world who make art with all kinds of different mediums, and you can too!

Goodbye!

Thank you for joining us on our art journey. We hope that this is just the beginning for you, and that you find inspiration to make your own art. The art world is full of so many stories and so many artists, but the most exciting story is *your* story. We can't wait to see the art you make! And remember: the most important thing is to make a start – put pen to paper, brush to canvas, hand to clay and start making art!

Permissions

Henri Matisse *The Snail*, Album/Scala, Florence

Piet Mondrian *Broadway Boogie Woogie*, Digital image, The Museum of Modern Art, New York/Scala, Florence

Frida Kahlo *Self Portrait with Monkeys*, Photo © Fine Art Images / Bridgeman Images

David Hockney *A Bigger Splash*, Permission given by David Hockney Studios

Roy Lichtenstein *Whaam!* Christie's Images, London/Scala, Florence

Hokusai *Under the Wave off Kanagawa*, H. O. Havemeyer Collection, Bequest of Mrs. H. O. Havemeyer, 1929, The Met

Banksy *Balloon Girl*, Courtesy of Pest Control Office, Banksy, 2004

Bridget Riley *To a Summer's Day*, © Bridget Riley 2025. All rights reserved.

Vincent van Gogh *Sunflowers*, Bridgeman Images

Romero Britto *Britto Garden*, Artwork created by world renowned artist, Mr. Romero Britto © 2000, Britto Central, Inc. All Rights Reserved.

Joan Miró *The Harlequin's Carnival*, Bridgeman Images

Giuseppe Arcimboldo *Vertumnus*, © 2025 Banco de México Diego Rivera Frida Kahlo Museums Trust, Mexico, D.F. / DACS

Diego Rivera *Dream of a Sunday Afternoon in Alameda Park*, Bridgeman Images

Jim Dine *Four Hearts*, (1969) © Tate, London / Art Resource, NY

Alexander Calder *Red Maze III*, © 2025 Calder Foundation, New York / DACS, London

Gwen John *The Convalescent*, © Fitzwilliam Museum / Bridgeman Images

Alberto Giacometti © 2025 Succession Alberto Giacometti / DACS

Henri Rousseau *Tiger in a Tropical Storm or Surprised!* Bridgeman Images

Frank Bowling *Dog Daze*, © Frank Bowling. All Rights Reserved, DACS 2023. Courtesy the artist.

Hilma af Klint *Altarpiece, No.1*, Bridgeman Images

Georgia O'Keeffe *Jimson Weed/White Flower No. 1*, Bridgeman Images

Robert Indiana *LOVE*, © 2025 Morgan Art Foundation Ltd. / Artists Rights Society (ARS), New York, DACS, London

Augusta Savage *The Harp*, New-York Historical Society, Purchase, Coaching Club Acquisition Fund

Jordan Casteel *Barbershop*, TBC

Nam June Paik *Electronic Superhighway: Continental U.S., Alaska, Hawaii (commonly called Electronic Superhighway, 2015)*, Smithsonian American Art Mus./Art Res

Lee Ufan *From Line*, Photo Smithsonian American Art Museum/Art Resource/Scala, Florence/© 2025 ADAGP, Paris and DACS, London

Emily Kam Kngwarreye *Awelye*, © 2025 Emily Kam Kngwarreye/Copyright Agency. Licensed by DACS

Antony Gormley *Royal Academy exhibition*, Artwork © Antony Gormley, Photograph by Oak Taylor-Smith

Jean-Michel Basquiat *Grillo*, © Estate of Jean-Michel Basquiat. Licensed by Artestar, New York.

Yayoi Kusama Lyon & Turnbull / Bridgeman Images

Andy Warhol *Marilyn Monroe*, © 2025 The Andy Warhol Foundation for the Visual Arts, Inc. / Licensed by DACS, London.

Andy Warhol *Endangered Species (complete set, 1983)*, © 2025 The Andy Warhol Foundation for the Visual Arts, Inc. / Licensed by DACS, London.

Tracey Emin *I Want My Time With You*, © Tracey Emin. All rights reserved, DACS 2025

Katherine Bernhardt *Pink*, Courtesy of CounterEditions.com and the Artist. © the Artist

Cassi Namoda *Little is Enough For Those with Love Mimi Nakupenda*, Courtesy Pippy Houldsworth Gallery, London. © Cassi Namoda 2025. Photo: Mark Blower.

Ramesh Mario Nithiyendran *Installation*, © Ramesh Mario Nithiyendran